BARBARA ROSE, Ph.D.

If GOD *Hears Me,* I WANT AN ANSWER!

R THE ROSE GROUP
Uplifting Humanity One Book at a Time ™

If God Hears Me, I Want an Answer!

The Rose Group
Uplifting Humanity One Book at a Time™
Florida, USA

ISBN10: 0974145750
ISBN13: 978-0-9741457-5-4

You may contact the author through her Web site,
www.borntoinspire.com

Cover and interior design and layout by
Words Plus Design, *www.wordsplusdesign.com*

Barbara Rose, Ph.D. logo design by
Georgia Wilson, *www.thedrawingroom.net.au*

Spirituality/ Personal Transformation
Self Help/ Personal Transformation
Answers from God
Spiritual Communication
Higher Self Communication

Also by Barbara Rose, Ph.D.

Dear God, I Have Teenagers. Please Help!
(Dear God Series™)

Dear God, How Do I Get Over a
Former Lover I Still Love?
(Dear God Series™)

Dear God, How Can I Learn to Love Myself?
(Dear God Series™)

Know Yourself: A Woman's Guide to Wholeness,
Radiance & Supreme Confidence

Stop Being the String Along:
A Relationship Guide to Being THE ONE

If God Was Like Man: A Message from God
to All of Humanity

Individual Power: Reclaiming Your Core,
Your Truth and Your Life

To all of the people I have worked with who showed me through their own profound personal transformations that this work is for real.

To *Bill Burns,* who told me about this before I ever knew it was even possible.

To Alan, who showed me over a period of five-and-a-half years that God's answers have always been pure truth and who has been the greatest catalyst in my life, for which I am eternally grateful.

To *You,* who—I know—can now begin the most profound transformation you have ever experienced, and for whom I pray it will be as deep and permanent as it still is for me.

Contents

Chapter 1 – In the Beginning, When You Are
Searching for Answers..1

Chapter 2 – When Life Brings You to Your Knees............4

How the Heart Opens Your Connection / 6
No Favorites / 7
Where Religion Comes into Play / 8
How You Hear God / 10
What You Can Learn from This Experience / 15
How the Answers Come to You / 15
Receiving Answers from God in Writing / 20
Purity of Motive / 21
Answers from God via Dreams / 24
Answers for Humanity / 26

Chapter 3 – When God Answers...28

How It Began / 29
No More Predictions / 35
Getting Connected / 36
Protecting Yourself / 38
The Greatest Questions to Ask / 41
How It Feels While You Receive Answers from God / 43
Highest Truth and Transformation / 45

Chapter 4 – How God's Answers Will
Transform Your Life 47

The Questions to Ask / 50
The Answers / 55
The Integration Process / 56

A Personal Example: From Tragedy to Seeing the
    Higher Perspective / 63
The Most Crucial Aspect of Asking for Answers / 65
When, Where, and How to Write / 67
On Sharing the Information You Receive with Others / 68
How to Know If It Is Coming from God / 70
When God's Answers Become a Catalyst for Global
    Change and Transformation / 72
Challenges and Society / 78
When People Are Afraid of Receiving the Truth
    from God / 88
No Interference from God / 90
Transforming Views of Self / 94

Chapter 5 - Receiving Answers from God for
Other People..100

How to Tell When Ego Has Taken Over / 110
When God Works Through You for Others / 113

About the Author 121

If GOD Hears Me, I WANT AN ANSWER!

Chapter 1

In the Beginning, When You Are Searching for Answers

There was a time in my life when the rug was pulled out from beneath me, and all I wanted was an answer from God.

There may have been a time in your life when your entire reality fell apart. Or you may have experienced deep injustice, pain, misfortune, or despair. Perhaps there was a time in your life, as in mine, when you felt so lost and filled with despair that you didn't want to wake up the next morning.

I would venture to say that just about every human being who lives on this earth has felt tremendous inner pain at one time or another.

I was guided by God to write this book, to share with you that no matter what situation you face, no matter how horrible the conditions in your life may appear to you, you *can* receive an answer directly from God, and you do not need anyone else to bring these answers to you.

For some, this may appear to be New Age. But throughout the history of humanity, all people have always sought answers when they couldn't figure them out on their own.

The purpose of this book is to teach you exactly how to receive the answers you seek. I will share how I do it, and I will give you simple guidance so that you know how to receive the answers, what to do, and what to look out for to ensure that the answers you receive are truly from God and not just from your own ego.

There is not a religion attached to this.

Everyone, from every religion and spiritual path, can receive answers directly from God. This information can be shared with anyone, of any age, beginning at age five. That might surprise you, but children can easily learn this. My deepest hope is that every member of the human race learns and understands that God does hear you. You *can* receive answers. And the very best time to receive them is when your heart truly wants them.

Let us now go through this process. By the end of this book, you too will know in no uncertain terms that you can receive the answers. There is one prerequisite, however, and that is that you truly have to ask from your heart.

Chapter 2

When Life Brings You to Your Knees

As I touched on in the previous chapter, there was a time when life brought me down to my knees. I experienced injustice in an unwarranted child-custody litigation suit. I adored my two children, as I still do, with all of my being and never once hit them or called them a negative name. As I was served with custody litigation papers, I couldn't believe my eyes. I did not have the funds to hire an attorney throughout the entire litigation process. As a result, I was completely railroaded, and I lost primary custody of my two small children. I was given visitation rights. That was many years ago, and at that time I felt as if my soul was ripped out from my being. I couldn't understand *how* this injustice could happen to me. I used to look up to the sky asking God, "Why? How could you let this happen to me? You know I never did anything wrong. Why, God, why? I want an answer!"

There might have been a time in your life when you also wanted an answer. There might be an event happening right now in your life that seems so unfathomable, so unjust, or so deeply tragic that you cannot believe it is actually happening to you.

When life brings you to your knees, when you feel so hopeless and helpless, so filled with disillusionment, you might feel that the only place you can look is to the sky, while you ask God why.

How the Heart Opens Your Connection

There is no greater motive in the universe than love.

The pain you feel in your heart, or the longing, or the fear, or the despair that makes you feel as if your heart is crushed acts like a conduit, providing one of the most profound ways to receive answers from God. And this is the first ground rule for receiving answers: the request must come from your heart. A prayer or request that comes so forcefully through your heart, with such a deep and earnest desire for an answer—that prayer or request is like a laser beam that reaches the highest realm in this universe. This is the realm of God, and within this realm, the energy of your heart is felt when your request is so strong.

No Favorites

God does not favor one human being over another. God does not play favorites. A heartfelt request can come from anyone. And it is during this heartfelt request that the answers are immediately given. This happens often with people who have made many mistakes. Perhaps their life is a complete mess. So they, too, turn to God and ask for answers.

Because God does not play favorites, even people who have previously lived lives in which they hurt others have been transformed once they sought answers from God. As a result, they were able to turn their lives around for the better.

For example, back in the 1960s when I was in the sixth grade, a man came to speak at our school to teach us about drug awareness. He used to deal drugs and had been arrested for the crimes he committed. He felt deep pain while in prison, realizing that his life had become everything other than what he wanted it to be. His heart opened. He wanted to transform his life for the better. He prayed to God for answers, and he received them. He then became a positive force in society by speaking to children in schools all over New York City to help prevent them from using drugs. He also worked with the police to help them find other people who were dealing drugs to kids in schoolyards. What was once a destructive life that many people would condemn became a positive force to prevent drug dealing and drug use. The man's greatest wrongs were transformed into a positive force to help children and society. God did not condemn him. Instead, God gave him positive guidance and direction because the man really wanted it from his heart. This shows that God does not play favorites. All people who are willing and able can ask God for an answer, for direction, clarification, and guidance about how to transform their lives for positive and lasting change.

Where Religion Comes into Play

Organized religion was in fact created by people. I would venture to say that before Moses was born, and before Jesus was born, and before Mohammed was born, and before Buddha was born, before all of them were born, there was no organized religion as we know it today.

Would you agree with this?

So let us now take the view that before organized religions were created by people, based on the people they loved, it was simply humanity and God.

And even now, with organized religions, there is still humanity and God.

Religions never took this connection away. No matter what religion you follow, and even if you do not follow a religion, you are still as connected to God as humanity was before the major religions were created.

It is important for you to understand this perspective; you need to know that you are a part of God whose spirit is inside of you with every breath you take, and religion can never take this connection away from you. Whether or not you follow a religion, it is not religion that gives you your connection to God. God works in you, as you, and through you at all times.

How You Hear God

Did you ever have a gut instinct? Did you ever hear an inner "still small voice"? Did you ever just have a feeling about something?

There has yet to be one human being I have spoken with who has said they regretted following their gut instincts. Moreover, there has yet to be one single human being I have spoken with who was glad they did *not* follow their gut instincts.

This is the beginning, the foundation of receiving answers from God. Although there are many more steps in the process, which I will describe in this book, I must start at the foundation of how to receive answers directly from God, easily, to make a significant difference in your life.

When you have a gut feeling, or a gut instinct, this is God communicating to you, guiding you, and even answering you. Even if you do not consciously ask a question, God is *always* guiding you in the direction toward your highest good.

You have six senses, not five. It is your sixth sense, which is the strongest sense of all, that is your direct connection to God.

Additionally, your sixth sense is the only one you can never lose. You can lose the five physical senses of sight, hearing, taste, touch, and smell, and still receive answers from God.

Your sixth sense cannot be measured or observed from the outside. Your sixth sense is the one and only sense you have that transcends all five of your other senses. No one can take this sixth sense away from you, and no one can give it to you. It is your built-in connection to God.

Additionally, your sixth sense will never lie to you or steer you in the wrong direction.

Let me ask you again now: Did you ever have a gut feeling? Did you ever follow it? Were you glad you did? I am certain you will answer yes to these questions.

When you have a gut feeling, it is vital that you follow it. Follow it no matter what your head tells you, no matter what anyone says to you, and no matter how things appear on the outside that might seem to contradict what your gut is telling you.

Perhaps you know this already, or perhaps you are still unsure about trusting and following your gut instincts.

For those of you who are more advanced in this awareness, please understand that many people are conditioned or taught to live only according to what their five senses show them. So it is important that I cover all aspects of receiving answers from God for all people, at all levels of spiritual awakening or consciousness awakening.

Now, at this beginning stage of receiving answers from God, I must share a true story with you so that you really understand how crucial the answers are that you receive from God as gut instincts.

Years ago, my mother, who lives on the west coast of Florida, was visiting me on the east coast of Florida. The road between the east and west coasts in Florida is called Alligator Alley.

When I woke up on the morning that I was supposed to drive her home, the words of God came into my mind, along with an incredibly strong feeling in my gut and in the middle of my chest. The words that came to me were, "Barbara, do not drive your mother back to the west coast today on Alligator Alley, because if you do, you will die, and your children will be without a mother."

My mother woke up and said that we should have some coffee and that I could drive her home in a couple of hours.

I knew from years of receiving information and answers from God that no matter what outer conditions look like, and no matter what anybody else says, I have to follow the guidance God gives me.

Here's what I told my mother: "Mom, I don't care what you say or how upset you are going to get, but God let me know that if I drive across Alligator Alley today to take you home, I will die and my children will be without a mother. So I will take you home tomorrow."

Now, the weather outside was beautiful. There was not a cloud in the sky. My mother was quite upset with me. She looked at me and said, "You know, Barbara, you're f____ crazy." To which I replied, "Mom, you can call me crazy, insane, anything you want. I will not go against what God told me because if I do, I will die. So I will take you back home tomorrow."

My mother called my father, who was at home on the west coast, and asked him to come pick her up. He said he would come and get her early in the afternoon. Then two hours later, at the exact time I would have been on Alligator Alley, the telephone rang in my house. It was my father. His sister was watching the news on the west coast of Florida, and she called my father and said: "I hope Barbara didn't leave yet because Alligator Alley is completely closed in both directions for the entire day. There was a terrible accident with many cars, and dead bodies lying on the lanes of incoming and ongoing traffic. The newscast said it was the worst car accident in the history of the state of Florida."

When my mother heard this, she said she would never doubt me again.

What You Can Learn from This Experience

The only reason I share this with you is to help you learn to trust that when you receive guidance, when words come into your mind, when you have a gut feeling, you must follow it as if God appeared in person and gave you this information—because it *is* God who is giving you this information and guidance via a "still small voice" and via your gut instincts. So please trust it and follow it, because it can very well save your life, just as it did for me.

How the Answers Come to You

People receive information, answers, warnings, and guidance from God in many ways. Without putting all of the labels on each level or area of this direct communication, I will simply share with you the most common ways.

Still Small Voice

This is an inner voice that is heard not by your ears as an audible sound but by your mind. You "hear" words as they come into your mind.

The words may say things such as "leave now" or "walk away" or "take this road home today instead of the one you usually travel."

Now, when this still small voice guides you, as I said earlier, it is God guiding you.

Let's use the last example: "Take this road home today instead of the one you usually travel." You hear it on the inside. And then, if you are not in the habit of following the still small voice unconditionally, your head may pop up with a doubt, such as, "Where did that come from? I always take the same road home. That was just my imagination." So if you listen to what your head, or ego on the personality level, is telling you rather than to God's still small voice, and if you take the road that your head told you to take, lo and behold, three minutes later there is a traffic jam or some inconvenience on the road you have chosen to travel based on *your* thoughts, and on your free will. And then you might say to yourself: "Something inside told me not to take this road home today, and I didn't listen. Now I'm sitting here stuck in traffic, when I have to get home to cook dinner for my children."

This is how the still small voice of God speaks to you. The good news is that once you are in the habit of following God's guidance via the still small voice, you can never go wrong! You are always guided, each moment. So I am guiding you to make God's still small voice *the* guiding voice of your life, for each moment you are alive.

Strong Internal Feelings

Another way God gives you answers is through your feelings. I am not speaking of emotions. I am speaking of what you can call a vibe or a strong internal sensation that makes you feel the energy about a person or circumstance throughout your stomach or chest area.

For example, when I receive an e-mail, I can "feel" the energy of the person from the e-mail. It either feels clear, clean, pure, and true in my chest and in my gut, or it feels negative or not pure or just not right. You must learn to trust these feelings completely. Your feeling, the very *first* instinctual feeling you have, is the one to trust, before your head comes up with doubts. The first feeling is the pure one that will never lead you astray. These feelings are your internal guideposts, and once you get into the habit of following them, your life will be filled with a lot more trust and inner peace.

Visions

Some people receive visions. Visions are pictures that come into your mind as vividly as if what you see in your mind is actually in front of you. A vision might be a picture of what a person you have never known looks like, or a picture of a future event that will come to pass in your life. Visions are seen within the mind's eye. They are another way God brings information to you, and they can serve to clarify situations or guide you in your life.

Visions come to people from God without warning, out of the blue. Either you get them or you don't. Some people get them regularly. Other people may have only a couple of visions in their lifetime.

Internal Hearing

Another word for internal hearing is "clairaudience," which refers to a greatly accelerated still small voice. With clairaudience, the voice is not so small; it is strong, certain, and filled with pure truth. And you "hear" it as words that come into your mind. As a matter of fact, every word that you are reading in this book came "through" me from God by the words that came into my mind, words I "heard" and simply wrote down exactly as I received them.

All human beings can hear God's guidance within their minds. You can view it as an advanced level of hearing God's still small voice in your mind. The only difference between this and God's "still small voice" is practice in listening and following it. Once you are so attuned to this and follow it unconditionally, it does become *the* guiding voice of your life. This takes me to the next level of how God gives you answers: in writing.

Receiving Answers from God in Writing

Many people have learned how to receive answers from God in writing because I taught them, just as I am now going to teach you. This will enable you to either completely transform your own life or receive an answer your heart longs for to a question about any situation facing you.

I must share with you that it is not me, Barbara, on the personality level, who teaches this to people. It is God. He sends the words into my mind, and I share them, either through writing or speech, to teach others. I do not do this work or share this process on my own accord from the five-sensory personality level. I cannot take credit for this because it comes from God, who works through me.

You, too, can bring through information from God—by writing down the words that flow into your mind—to make a significant difference not only in your own life but for humanity. Each one of my books is written "through" me and not "from" me.

This is *not* automatic writing. There is nothing automatic about it. God doesn't just take over your being without your asking for the answers or information to flow through you in writing.

You have free will and choice. You can start and stop a writing at any time. You can ask God to bring you answers via your writing anywhere, at any time, and for any reason, so long as your motive is pure.

Purity of Motive

The second ground rule for receiving answers from God is that your motive must be pure. By purity of motive I mean that the purpose of your request for answers or information must be solely to help or serve either yourself or others, and that you are not trying to control or cause harm to others on any level. The motive must be 100 percent pure. This is the only way you will receive answers from God. I must elaborate on this, and then I will give you examples of the kinds of questions to ask.

Let's say you had a quarrel with a loved one, and you really want to resolve it and come to peace with the other person.

You can write something like, "Dear God, Please guide me as to what to do or what to say with Jane so that we can resolve our conflict and have peace between us." This is a pure motive. It is to bring peace to a situation, and you *will* receive the answers from God in the form of words that flow into your mind. As the words come into your mind in the form of an answer to your question, you simply write them down verbatim, without censoring anything. Then when you re-read what you brought through from God, you should feel uplifted by the higher perspective you received.

Here is an example of a motive that is not pure: "Dear God, I know my neighbor comes and goes at all hours of the night. What is she doing?"

Why is this motive not pure? Because you are minding your neighbor's business, which has nothing to do with you, and your *heart* is not seeking an answer to create positive, life-renewing change or transformation.

How to Know Whether Your Motive Is Pure

The only way to know whether your motive is pure and from the heart is to ask yourself whether you would like it if someone else requested the same information involving you, and for the same reason. So if you had a quarrel with a loved one or a friend, and he or she did a writing requesting guidance from God because he or she truly wanted to have a peaceful resolution, this would not bother you. Perhaps your friend just needs to find inner peace about you and asked God how to do this. I believe this would be okay with you.

On the other hand, would you like your neighbor to do a writing just to snoop into your life to find out what you were doing? I believe you would not like this. So the rule "do unto others as you would have them do unto you" lets you determine whether your motive is pure.

In the next chapter, I am going to give you in great detail all you need to know to bring through answers from God. Before I do this, I must cover one more area: receiving information from God in your sleep.

Answers from God via Dreams

Many times when our personalities are in flux, and we are trying so hard to figure out the answers, we find that the answers are given to us in our dreams. This happens to all people. The saying "I'll sleep on it" indicates that during sleep, people receive a fresh perspective about the concerns weighing on their hearts and minds. When you go to bed feeling upset, unsure, or puzzled, and then wake up with an answer or a clear perspective about the situation you felt uncertain about before going to sleep, you can be sure that the clearer perspective was given to you by God to help you in your life.

I have seen firsthand accounts of people who received answers in their sleep to questions that came from their hearts, and these were people who did not believe that God existed.

As I said earlier, God does not play favorites. Just as a loving parent purely and unconditionally loves a child even when that child grows into a rebellious teenager, so it is with God. You will receive an answer in your sleep to help you in your life. Perhaps you already have. One of the greatest things you can do when you are at the beginning stages of consciously seeking answers from God is to ask for an answer or a realization or a clearer perspective to come into your mind during your sleep, so that when you wake up, you will have clarity and the positive guidance and direction you need to work toward your highest good and the highest good of all concerned.

Answers for Humanity

Many times, people face situations such as illness, injustice, tragedies, and hardships that countless other people also face.

There is a higher reason why we face these situations. It is so that they can be transformed, both for the people they personally affect and for the masses.

When we face a specific life challenge, we are usually given two options. The first is to remain a victim. The second is to rise from within and create positive transformation because of the challenge.

So if you are going through a challenge in your life, and if you want to know whether God hears you, and if you want an answer, the next chapter will show you exactly what to do, what to ask, and how to receive the answers you are seeking to transform any area of your life, from the smallest to the largest. God does not put a minimum or a limit on what you can ask or on the answers you will receive.

There is no limit. It is time for you to know that God does hear you. It is time for you to receive the answers you want.

So turn the page and let's begin the greatest process that can transform anything and everything in your life exactly as it has done in mine.

Chapter 3

When God Answers

I t is important at this time that you know where I'm coming from, and that you know I am a regular human being just like you. So I am going to share with you how this all happened. How I learned about the process of getting answers from God, and the doubts, fears, and insecurities I went through. Everyone I have taught this process to went through the same thing.

How It Began

In 1994, I had a session with a highly spiritually evolved man named Bill Burns. He told me that I had the ability to bring through information from my Higher Self. I asked, "What's a Higher Self?" He said, "Your Higher Self is the one you call God."

I literally laughed in his face and said, "Are you kidding me? Why would God want to talk to me? I'm not Mother Teresa or the Dalai Lama. Why would God want to speak to me?" He said, "You can't understand or relate to this now. It's not like you're going to be some Madam Zelda with a scarf on your head and a crystal ball, but you will see that you will bring through information from God in your writings and in speech to uplift the spiritual consciousness of humanity."

I looked at him as if he was from Pluto. Although I had deep respect for him, and do to this day, I didn't understand what he was talking about, and I certainly did not believe that I could receive direct answers from God.

But I was curious. So I went home and did a writing: I asked God questions in writing and wrote down the answers I received as the words flowed into my mind. Even though I received answers that all turned out to be true, I dismissed the whole thing. I thought I was probably making it all up.

Then, life happened. Hardships happened. Injustice happened. A relationship happened, and I fell in love.

Now, if anything is going to get a person to really start asking God for answers, it is when he or she is in deep turmoil. I was writing letters to God every single day; many times, two, three, four, and even five times a day. I didn't understand why the events in my life were happening. I didn't know what to do or how to figure everything out, and I wanted answers!

I received tens of thousands of pages of answers. The only problem was my ego. I did not believe the answers were really coming from God. I kept thinking I was making it all up. Then I began to receive predictions. They were all on the personal level. Exact dates and times by which things would happen, all in advance. This happened for two solid years. During that time I seriously thought I had gone mad. I used to walk around the house and say to myself, "I must be insane. I'm probably just a harmless psychopath." I really thought I was going crazy. I didn't believe that the one God, creator of Heaven and Earth, would actually communicate directly with me.

So then in my writings I would ask for another prediction. It came true. Then another, and another. At one point, the words that flowed into my mind from God were, "Barbara, when will you finally believe? How many predictions do you need to come to pass?" And I would write, "Dear God, please just give me one more, and then I will believe." So I received yet another one. But I still didn't believe. This went on for two solid years. I was a tough nut to crack. Then I would write, "Dear God, what is going to happen this week?" I received another prediction. Once again, God brought the words into my mind that I wrote down verbatim. The words were, "When will you believe?" So I once again wrote, "Okay God, just one more prediction and then I will believe." This was after receiving hundreds of them. So I received another prediction with the exact date and the latest time by which the event would occur on that date. For example, I was in a long, deep, and emotionally difficult relationship with a man I dearly loved and still do. He broke up with me, for about the twentieth time, and said that it was "over forever." I really believed him because he sounded dead serious. I had even reached the point that I thought I had wanted it to be over forever. Then I wrote to God and asked, "Dear God, is the relationship really over? Please tell me it's over, I can't take it anymore. If it is, I can handle it. Please tell me the truth." The answer I received was, "No, it is not over. He will call you to see you on Wednesday by 6:00 p.m." After two solid years of predictions, when that one came to pass (I received a call from him on Wednesday at 5:30 p.m. saying that he wanted to see me), my ego gave way as if a dam had burst open. I finally believed I was not making it all up.

Logically, I had to conclude that there was no way on this earth that I could come up with advance information documented for two solid years and be correct each and every time.

So I believed. But I had tremendous fear about what other people would think of me. I feared being viewed as some kind of New Age fruitcake. I feared how I would be viewed by society.

It was through my writings, and all of the information I received from God in my writings, that I was able to completely transform my entire life.

I had lost everything. There was a time I didn't have a home, a car, or money for food, and my life was at the bottom of the barrel. My self-esteem and self-confidence were also at the bottom of the barrel.

God guided me in writing after writing about self-love, self-value, how to transform my life, what to do next, what to create, what to share, and what to write in books for humanity. God's words flow into my mind, and I write them down verbatim. The process feels exactly like taking dictation. The only difference is that rather than hearing the words spoken out loud by someone, the words come into my mind silently, so it is like taking internal dictation. What I mean by "internal" is that I hear the words within my mind, exactly as you might hear God's still small voice within your mind saying something such as "take this road home today instead of the one you usually take."

The process of personal transformation was given to me by God through my writings, and I can guarantee that if there is any area or aspect of your life in which you would like to see, feel, and experience positive transformation, God will give you every answer in your own writings exactly as He or She does for me and for the countless other people I have taught this to who also receive direct answers from God every day of their lives.

It is also important for you to know that no matter *what* is upsetting you or what you may feel unsure about—even if you are not sure about the perfect words to say in reply to an e-mail—if it is important to you in your heart, you can ask God in writing for the perfect words to write, and then simply write down the answers as the words flow into your mind.

This is the beauty of the process. You can receive answers for anything that matters to you in your everyday life. You do not have to wait for an emergency. Here's a good rule of thumb: if you're not sure about something, ask God! There is one exception, however, and that is asking for predictions about future outcomes.

No More Predictions

Once I truly believed God was, in fact, communicating directly with me, God let me know that there would be no more predictions, because life is meant to be lived in the moment.

We will *always* receive a warning to keep us out of danger, and that warning comes in the moment, when we need it.

Predictions are for insecure people (and I was definitely one of them) who need assurances because they do not trust that all works out for their highest good, and they do not believe that the miracles in life unfold in the moment.

The most empowering thing you can feel is pure inner peace and trust while living in the moment, now, and following the next indicated step, as opposed to worrying about how everything is going to turn out. Everything is going to turn out for your highest good.

Getting Connected

Now you know the doubts, insecurities, and fears I felt when I began receiving guidance directly from God in my own writings. I feel deeply humbled and joyful to be able to share this process with you so that you, too, can receive all of the answers you need in order to propel your life forward in the most positive way.

First, the connection to God comes from your heart. All you need is a pure motive and a heartfelt desire for an answer.

Second, all you need to do to receive answers from God in writing is to take out a pen and paper and write your questions coming from the deepest place in your heart. This is the most crucial part of writing to God for answers. As the answers come into your mind, write them down exactly as you receive them, without censoring anything. Since you will not remember everything you wrote when you finish writing, it is important that you read the answers you wrote down. You can look at the answers at any time and re-read them. This is especially helpful when you are trying to transform an aspect of your life such as self-worth, or working through fears of making positive life changes. You can continue to re-read the answers you have received that were especially helpful to you until everything sinks in and the transformations you are working through have been completed. Re-reading the answers will always bring you a feeling of inner peace.

There are, however, certain things I do that I must share with you to make sure you are divinely protected and actually establish a pure connection; you want to be sure that the answers are coming *through* you from God and not *from* you on the personality or ego level.

⚬⚭⚬

Protecting Yourself

Whether or not this makes any sense to you now, I am obligated to make sure that you are divinely protected and receive information only from God and not from anyone else. God may also be called Holy Spirit, Higher Self, All That Is, Divine Source, or Creator. Whatever name you personally feel most comfortable with when referring to God is perfectly fine. People who are Christian might say Holy Spirit; people who are Muslim might say Allah. All of the names refer purely to God.

Ask either out loud or silently within your mind that you are consciously connected to God *only*. You can say or think something like this: "I want to be consciously connected to God, my Higher Self, the Holy Spirit, Christ Consciousness, God only of divine purest white light. I ask that my channel of communication is open to God and that I receive divine, pure, and perfect truth from God to help me (or to help someone else), for my highest good and the highest good of all."

Ask for divine white light, pink light, and purple light to surround you and protect you.

Now, I know this sounds like New Age woo woo, but asking for divine light to surround you and protect you will do just that. People have asked me about what the three colors of light represent. Someone once taught me that white light is pure divine protection. Pink light represents love. Purple light is also known as the violet flame and is representative of Archangel Michael. Asking for three layers of divine light to surround you protects you from negative energy coming from other people. Any negative energy is absorbed into the light and not into you. I am not an expert on the light spectrum, and this is all I know about it. I think that asking for extra protection can only be positive. It will certainly never hurt you.

Additionally, you can ask for your guardian angels to surround you and protect you.

Why do you need protection? You may wonder this, so here is the answer. When you open up your sixth sense and receive information that comes through you, you don't want just anyone out there in the universe to come through. You want only God to come through. It is like having the door to your house open; you don't want just any passerby to walk in. The same is true for receiving spiritual communication. You want to make sure that you are protected.

It is important that you know exactly who you are connecting to. When you pick up the telephone and call a friend, you don't just close your eyes and randomly punch numbers on the phone. You are careful to punch the numbers that will connect you to that specific person.

There are people, beautiful souls, who teach you how to connect to other beings in the universe such as angels or loved ones who have crossed over to the other side. But my purpose is to teach you how to connect directly with God, to whom all beings in the universe are connected.

When you look back over a period of days, weeks, months, or years and see the profound and incredible difference this connection has made in your life as a result of all of the answers you have received, you will know with absolute certainty that God speaks directly to you, exactly as He or She did to any person in whose name any of our modern day organized religions began, from the time of Moses and thereafter.

The Greatest Questions to Ask

Okay, you have asked for divine protection. Now, all you need to do is write "Dear God," and then write down any question from your *heart,* any question for which you want an answer, guidance, direction, clarification, understanding, or a higher perspective.

Simply write the questions in your own words, from your heart. God hears you from your heart. You connection *to* God is in your heart, not your head, your heart.

After you write down your questions, write some form of a thank-you. Personally, I write, "Thank you for Divine, Pure, and Perfect Truth in Advance, Love, Barbara."

You may phrase your thank-you in any way you like. It is important to feel gratitude because you are about to receive answers from God to help you with the questions you are asking from your heart.

Then, after you write your questions and thank-you, take seven deep breaths. This is important to relax you. Breathing also connects you to God.

Breathe deeply, so that the air goes deep into your belly. It doesn't matter if you breathe in through your nose or mouth, but do exhale from your mouth.

After you take seven deep breaths, or even as you take them, you will notice words flowing into your mind in the form of an answer to the questions you have written.

Write down every single word that flows into your mind. Don't censor the words. They might come very quickly, or slowly, but no matter how quickly or slowly the words come, and whether or not the words make sense to you as they flow into your mind, please just write them all down.

At some point the writing will come to a natural finish. As soon as the answers stop, go back and re-read everything you received.

How It Feels While You Receive Answers from God

While God answers you, you will feel inner peace. You will experience a loving and soothing feeling.

You will be completely aware of your surroundings. You will not go into some kind of zoned-out state. You will be conscious and aware, yet simultaneously deeply engaged in the moment as the words come into your mind.

Your handwriting may look different, and it may be difficult for you to read certain words. The *only* reason this is happening is because you will be writing faster than usual, so the words may look a bit sloppier than they would if you were consciously writing with the intention of perfect penmanship.

You can start and stop your writing at any time. For example, if you are expecting an important phone call or a package delivery and the telephone or the doorbell rings, you can stop the writing, attend to the phone call or visitor at your door if you choose to, and then pick up the writing where you left off.

You cannot *lose* your connection to God because this connection exists within you with every breath you take.

If you were interrupted and you want to pick up from where you left off, then take a few deep breaths and simply ask God to please continue to bring you the answers.

There is one thing you will *never* feel when God is answering you: you will never feel anything negative. You will never feel judged or condemned. You will feel unconditional love, incredible patience, peace, and acceptance; and you will feel supported.

God will never interfere with your free will and choice. You will always be guided toward what is for your highest good, and you will always be supported in what you truly wish for in terms of your life direction.

You will receive the highest truth in your answers, which are given to you so that you can live according to that truth rather than according to what your head tells you or what your fears tell you.

Highest Truth and Transformation

Something incredible happens when you start to receive answers from God: your highest and deepest truth will begin to surface. While this is authentically empowering, it can feel scary to the ego.

It is not always easy to live our highest truth and walk our talk. If you are searching for inner peace, however, the *only* way you will ever feel it is when you are, in fact, living your highest and deepest truth on all levels of your life.

In the next chapter, I am going to guide you so that you can actually see the most profound and incredible transformation with respect to any area of your life in which you feel something other than inner peace.

Turn the page and the answers will be there for you.

❦

Chapter 4

How God's Answers Will Transform Your Life

Direct communication with God brings the most power-ful, empowering, and tremen-dously transforming wisdom and guidance to all of humankind, unconditionally, purely, and without favoring one person over another.

There is no greater power in this uni-verse than love and truth. Your free will and choice plays a big role in receiving answers from God. You have to really want the answers because you deeply desire to turn around any aspect or view of yourself or your life for the better. When you feel determined, you will consciously choose to ask God for guidance and answers. This must be combined with a deep, heartfelt desire to become aware of your deepest truth, to live your life as your highest expression of self, and to transform anything that is either consciously or unconsciously holding you back. No matter how miserable your life may be or how terrible your view of yourself is, it can be transformed by receiving direct answers from God.

Another reason your determination to receive truth is so important is because you must feel an unquenchable desire to follow through on the truth you receive in your answers. This has nothing to do with judgment by God, because God judges no one. This pertains to following through on your deepest truth because doing so will free you from the pain of your past and from your fears. As I shared earlier, following through—acting on God's guidance—is not always easy! I know how difficult it was to receive guidance from God that I knew deep in my heart was for my highest good (such as not allowing myself to be treated like dirt) and how difficult that was before I developed genuine self-esteem. Living your truth has to be more important to you than living your fears. Bringing out the greatest you have within you has to be more important to you than remaining a victim and believing you can't live as your greatest expression of self.

Once you are deeply committed to transforming anything that has previously held you back, you will begin to feel that God is your partner. You will learn that you are an expression of God. You will know that you are never separate from God. Can you hear yourself breathe? God is that close, inside of you.

You see, there is one thing you can be certain of: Your Higher Self, God, *is* the anchor of truth within you, working as you and through you to enable you to transform any difficulty you are facing and to overcome any challenge that is in front of you.

There has yet to be a person on earth who truly and earnestly desired to bring about authentic personal transformation with God's direct guidance who hasn't done so.

Every day people send me messages and letters filled with the deepest gratitude about how receiving answers from God has transformed their life within *weeks*.

Now it is your turn. God answers you directly when you ask. God hears your pleas, your questions, and your concerns. God knows *how* to guide you in a way you can understand, in a way that will resonate within your heart, so that you feel both guided and unconditionally supported during times of doubt, confusion, fear, despair, and pain.

God's only purpose is to see you become a beacon of His or Her light, the unique and incomparable essence of who you are, which is All That Is in physical form.

To guide you through the process of formulating your questions, I will now give you some suggestions.

The Questions to Ask

When you are facing a difficult or painful situation, here are key questions

that will bring you core-level truth from
God in your writings.

1. Dear God, Can you please give me the
higher perspective concerning this situation and the higher reason why this is happening so I can better understand it?

2. Dear God, I feel fear of moving out of
my old situation and into the new one.
Can you please tell me what I am not seeing and what the underlying unconscious
fears are, so that I can become consciously
aware of them and transform them?

3. Dear God, How can I begin to view
myself in a way that enables me to feel
good enough and worthy?

4. Dear God, Can you please help me
learn how to let go of attachment to outcomes so that I can learn how to live with
inner peace?

5. Dear God, How can I release the emotional pain I feel from the circumstance in
my life that is happening now? How can I
view the situation from the highest perspective so that I can feel free from emotional pain and turmoil?

6. Dear God, Please help me to understand why I still feel stuck. Please help me have the courage to live my truth. How can I do this? Please give me the answers and let me know how.

7. Dear God, Why do I feel fear of being judged by other people and worry about what they are going to think of me? How can I transform this?

8. Dear God, I feel so alone without a partner. Can you please tell me how to feel complete, even when I don't have someone right now to share my life with?

9. Dear God, I do not understand how to trust the answers I receive from you in my writings. I think I am making it all up. Can you *please* help me to know how I can tell if it is coming from you or from just me?

10. Dear God, How can all of this be happening to me? What is the higher reason? How can I see the higher perspective? What am I supposed to be learning from this experience?

11. Dear God, Why are people judging me, and how can I release my need to feel

that I have to explain myself to them to get their approval or understanding?

12. Dear God, When I set the intention to manifest something, and it does not happen, can you please help me to understand why? What is the higher reason for this right now in my life?

13. Dear God, Why, after so much work on myself, do I still feel insecure? What does it take to feel inner security and inner peace? Can you please give me the answers so I truly have a realization now?

14. Dear God, Why have I been experiencing physical illness? Is there something inside that I am not seeing or a reason why? Can you please help me to see whatever I am not seeing so I can get better?

15. Dear God, I have tried so hard to feel that you are really answering me, and sometimes I still feel afraid of following the truth I receive from you. Can you please tell me how to overcome my fear of really following my truth in my life?

16. Dear God, There are many times I feel good, and now I feel myself changing. I am losing interest in doing the things I used to

do and in associating with my friends. I'm not sure how to handle this, or what to say. Can you please give me the answers and guide me?

17. Dear God, I would like to write a book to help people. Is it possible that you can write the book through me in my journal so it truly helps humanity?

18. Dear God, My boyfriend [girlfriend] broke up with me, and I feel terrible. Please tell me how to overcome this pain. How can I view this situation and see what is for my highest good? How can I get out of the deep pain and misery I feel? Please guide me!

19. Dear God, I was raised in a religion that taught me differently about you. Why don't you judge people who do things wrong? Why do people do things wrong, and why do I feel as if I am doing something wrong by asking you for answers? Why would you want to answer *me*?

20. Dear God, I am trying to figure out an answer to the project I am working on. Can you *please* give me the answer so I can get a good night sleep?

The questions I have been given to bring you in this chapter are questions that can apply to any person, situation, or state of being while living life on the earth.

The Answers

The answers you receive from God will help you *in the moment,* concerning any situation you are facing. The answers will be simple, yet filled with deep truth. You will feel a strong sense of unconditional, pure love, and you will feel a lot more inner peace after you read the answers you have received.

One of the most important aspects of writing your questions to God is knowing that the answers you receive will uplift you and bring you a higher perspective. You will be given the view that comes from the highest realm, the realm where your heart and soul are always connected. That is the realm of God, who is your Higher Self.

The perspective you receive will enable you to dramatically shift your views, which will then enable you to dramatically shift any area of your life from the inside out.

You will receive clarity. You will receive certainty. You will receive only truth. And when you do, it is important for you to re-read the answers any time you feel a lack of inner peace concerning that area until it is completely transformed. As your perspective is transformed, you will feel more courage to integrate the changes you desire to make concerning your view of self and any area of your life. As your perspective changes, you will begin to feel more inner peace.

The Integration Process

When you embark on personal transformation, the process takes time to integrate. The more earnestly you desire the transformation, the more God will work with you. You will receive great clarity in your writings. You will become more aware of your feelings and your truth. You will be given astounding guidance moment by moment. And during your sleep you will receive additional help, support, guidance, and answers. If you are going through an especially difficult time emotionally, one of the best things you can do is write a deeply heartfelt letter to God before you go to sleep and ask that clarity, inner peace, and resolution to be given to you.

When you wake up, you will actually have life-altering realizations that you have never previously experienced. You will wake up with pure inner peace.

When your heart is so deeply committed with the pure motive of love to uplift and transform, you will be guided moment by moment as ideas suddenly come into your mind from God. The greatest thing you can do is *follow through* on the guidance and ideas you receive when you receive them. As you follow through in your *actions*, you are simultaneously transforming old, self-limiting patterns and becoming your highest expression of self. As a result, you may very well make a positive and lasting difference in our world.

The whole purpose of life on earth is to become and shine as your God-Self. It is important for you to remember that there is no separation between you and God.

God is not sitting on a throne in Heaven watching you, judging you, and sentencing you to hell. God only wishes to uplift you, so that you feel the oneness you actually are; and as you do, your life will feel like a moment-by-moment serene joy. It *is* heaven on earth. As I shared earlier, it is important for you to remember that when God answers you, it might feel difficult for you to actually follow through with the answers. This is okay as it is simply the process of transformation from the ego-separate view into the I AM oneness view, in which you actually begin to know, see, feel, and believe that it is you and God—you as God, and God as you.

If you feel difficulty in living your truth and in following through in your actions, please give yourself a lot of unconditional love, patience, and understanding as well as compassion. This is what you will always receive from God, and this is what you must always give to yourself.

Writing to God about your feelings *while you are experiencing them*—feelings

such as fear, frustration, anger, jealousy, bit-
terness, despair, loneliness, longing, or
worry—and asking God to help you
understand your feelings will bring you
greater clarity. Those feelings can be transformed as a result of the clarity you receive
in your answers from God.

You might have noticed the one question that was not suggested in this chapter:
this pertains to an outcome.

You see, when you are attached to an
outcome, then you live with a lot of anxi-
ety. The key to living a life of inner peace
on earth is to trust that God is *always*
answering you in the moment. As you are
guided moment by moment, you will feel
greater trust. As you feel greater trust, you
will "go with the flow," and you will be
guided by God every instant of your life.
When you live life in *this* way, there is no
possibility of an outcome not turning out
for your highest good. Everything *will* turn
out for your highest good as you consciously become one with God, and know that
this *is* your spiritual nature. Your spiritual
nature can and will transcend and transform any and every aspect of human nature

that is still directed by ego on the personality level, which is run completely by fear.

If you recall, earlier in this book it was written that there will be no more predictions. Much more empowering than predictions are guidance and realizations concerning what weighs on your heart and in your mind in this moment, rather than living in fear concerning the future.

It has been said that on the other side, in the dimension that people call Heaven, or the higher dimensions, there is no such thing as time. All is now. All is simultaneous, and nothing is predestined.

Outcomes are the result of your intention, focus, and conscious choice in the moment. If you are living in fear about the future, God will *always* bring you comfort and reassurance as well as perfect guidance as to how to view your situation in the now moment, along with the best steps to take toward your highest good.

It is crucial for you to see that attachment to outcomes is more disempowering than trust and living with certainty, faith, and belief as you live your truth in the moment. Naturally, one moment will lead you to the next.

When you try to plan it all out, and then worry about how your plans are going to turn out, this detracts from the joy you can feel from the process of your life, as you live and express that which brings your heart the deepest and purest joy based on pure motives. Additionally, worrying disempowers you, keeps you stuck in fear, and blocks the positive guidance you can receive in the moment that will guide you toward your highest good. When your mind is focused on receiving positive guidance from God, then it will flow into your mind. Whenever you *do* find yourself worrying, immediately take a few deep breaths and ask God to bring you guidance. Then your mind will be open and receptive. As a result, you will receive positive guidance, worry will be replaced with clarity, and you will feel a lot better.

Many times you will receive answers that guide you to trust, and to love yourself. Many people have difficulty with self-love. The "higher" reason for this is so that your view of self can be transformed from the inside out. When God gives you the answers, and you feel the purity and truth of those answers, you will begin to love the transformational process you feel on the inside. You will begin to feel more secure because you will know that you are never alone. God is with you 24/7. And as love is your essence, your heartfelt desire to transform any view of self that is not based on love will be transformed when you ask God for answers, for the higher perspective, and for guidance to carry it out in your life, one moment at a time.

Whether you follow the answers God gives you is up to your free will and choice. Perhaps you are taking your life in a new direction and feel afraid of moving out of the old circumstances you have been living in. Or you might be in love and have many fears at the same time. The fears are a natural part of uprooting the old views as you move into your truth.

You will feel yourself growing in compassion as well as in courage—the courage to be and to express your highest essence as you share that essence through your unique and heartfelt contributions to yourself and to this world.

You will come to see the higher reason for any situation your personality views as deeply painful or tragic. You will come to know and feel the perspective God has, and as you earnestly ask for answers concerning any life situation, you will begin to feel a renewed sense of hope. You will begin to see things from the higher vantage point. This will enable you to rise above emotional pain and sorrow. It will also help others to rise by virtue of your sharing your process with those who ask you about it.

A Personal Example: From Tragedy to Seeing the Higher Perspective

I would like to share an example from my own life, an example in which my personality viewed a situation as so tragic that I nearly took my own life. The answers I received from God completely changed my perception, and I immediately shifted inside from feeling and being suicidal to feeling a deep understanding, renewed hope, and inner peace.

Many years ago, as I briefly shared earlier regarding the child-custody situation I experienced, I felt the deepest emotional pain that is more than I can express in words. Back then, as I viewed the situation, my perspective was that I had lost my children. I wrote letters to God asking for answers. I asked God how he could let me lose my children. God answered with the following: "You did *not* '*lose*' your children. You are merely sharing in the physical care for them with their father. You will always be their mother, and you will always be close to them. They are alive and will always be in your life. Please shift your view from *loss* to *sharing* the physical care for them."

When I received that perspective from God, I honestly and literally was instantaneously transformed within my mind. All of the despair was suddenly lifted. I realized this was, in fact, the truth! God's answer to me gave me a renewed sense of life as well as a renewed sense of even wanting to *be* alive. I then began to transform my entire life from scratch.

How can you put a price on an inner transformation from God? It is priceless, and it is free. You, just like me, will always receive the answers to your heartfelt questions. You will always receive the higher perspective.

The Most Crucial Aspect of Asking for Answers

The most crucial aspect of asking for answers from God is that you do it in the moment when you truly desire an answer because you want to understand and uplift yourself when you feel inner pain, confusion, turmoil, fear, or despair.

It is so vastly important that you get into the habit of taking out your pad and pen, writing to God, and asking for answers whenever you *do* feel upset. The point is that you want to receive the answers—the higher perspective—right away instead of remaining in misery.

There is no reason on earth to remain in misery, confusion, or turmoil when you can receive resolution, guidance, clarification, direction, and answers *now.*

When you feel pain or emotional upset, this is when it is crucial for you to write to God for answers.

You will find, as I have found, that just re-reading the answers you have been given will uplift your heart, your spirit, your perceptions, and your mind into a higher understanding where inner peace dwells and replaces confusion and despair.

Why wait? Why try to figure it all out on your own? Why go to others for answers when you can receive them directly from God?

I promise you that you will receive the clarity and direction you seek when you write to God and ask for it.

When, Where, and How to Write

The best way to write and bring through the answers from God is with a pen and notebook. It's especially important because you can bring through the answers any time, any place, and under any circumstance when you do it in handwriting, with a pen. The answers flow more easily, and you can do a writing in the park, on a mountain, at the beach, in a restroom, in your bedroom, anywhere, and at any time.

Writing by hand is the best option for bringing through the information. If you want to transcribe your writings afterwards and type them out to save them, this is perfectly fine. It is advisable that you type out the words as they flow into your mind only if you cannot physically write by hand. If you are not able to use your hands for writing or typing, then it is okay to speak the words into a recording device. Close your eyes when you do this, and simply say the words as they flow into your mind. You can always re-read or re-listen to the answers you receive.

It is important for you to keep your writings until the time comes when you truly feel you no longer want them because all you were previously going through has been completely transformed.

Many times, you can do a writing and ask God to help you just to get through this one day when you feel stuck. The process of transformation not only is deep but also permanent.

On Sharing the Information You Receive with Others

The only time it is advisable to share the answers you receive from God with others is when you truly desire to do so, and when the other person is open and receptive to hearing the information.

It is not advisable to share the information you receive with others to try to prove a point, or to get them to "open up" spiritually, because this would be forcing your desires on their own free will and choice.

Moreover, you do not have to prove yourself to anyone. You do not have to read the answers you receive to anyone if you do not wish to do so.

If you are in a relationship and are writing asking for understanding about the other person to help bring you clarity and more peace, share those writings with the other person only if they truly want to hear them. If they feel resistant, it is best to let them be and not try to force the answers you received from God on them.

When you place a steel cover over soil and then pour water on the steel cover, expecting it to be absorbed by the soil and the seeds planted in it, you will be disappointed. The water will simply bounce off the steel. It is the same with people. If they are not open, receptive, and truly *willing* and even desiring to hear what you bring through, then it will just bounce off them.

The purpose of your writings is for *your* personal growth and transformation, not the transformation of others.

If other people are not open to this level of communication with God, allow them to simply be. They will evolve and grow in their own time and in their own way.

Trying to force them to use this approach when they are not open to it will most likely not have the result you desire. The key is to live and let live. This is important, both for you and for them. Perhaps others do not believe, just as I did not believe many years ago that God would communicate directly with me. I had to learn, evolve, and grow at my own rate, in my own time, just as everybody else does. So please keep this in mind when you are eager to share your writings.

How to Know If It Is Coming from God

There are a few ways you will be able to tell whether your answers are coming from God or from your ego on the five-sensory personality level. One way is to see if you feel a deep sense of inner peace and love. Another way is to see if the answer truly brought you a higher perspective. If you feel this, then the answers are coming from God.

If you are still unsure, you can always log on to the IHSC, the Institute of Higher Self Communication message forum on Yahoo! Groups, which is free online. (To subscribe, send an e-mail to H i g h e r S e l f C o m m u n i c a t i o n - subscribe@yahoogroups.com.) There you will find a very pure group of supportive people from all over the world. You can ask questions, even post your writing, and ask one of the faculty members to read your post. They will "feel" the energy of your writing and immediately know whether your answers are from God. Everyone will be completely honest with you. Whenever I am able, I log on to the Higher Self Communication message forum on Yahoo! Groups and personally answer posts to be of help and service. This is a free, spiritual, global service that God guided me to create specifically for this reason: to give people a free and safe forum to turn to during their process of learning how to receive answers from God and a place from which they can receive support during times of personal crisis or uncertainty. It is a beautiful group that honors all human beings equally, and it has only one rule: all posts must come purely from the heart.

When God's Answers Become a Catalyst for Global Change and Transformation

When God brings you answers that serve to uplift you and your life, you will feel a certain amount of gratitude. You will feel awakened and inspired. As a byproduct of this joy, you may decide to go a step further. You may ask God to bring you information that can serve to both uplift and help humanity.

Depending on the purity of your desire, when your motive is so heart centered, when your only motive is to make a positive difference, you will find that you can ask God to bring through the information via a song, a book, artwork, a new paradigm for educating people, a resolution in the area of health care, the environment, and so on.

You will receive the answers as they come into your mind, and you can then bring them out as your own unique contribution to help life on earth from your heart. When you do this, no matter what field of work you are in, you will discover the indescribable inner peace that comes from serving in this manner. The inner peace you will feel is the result of living so purely in the moment. The joy comes from your expression of God through you, and the joy is felt when you see that what you have brought through is, in fact, making a positive difference.

The joy becomes priceless. No longer are you caught in the shackles of living in a dead-end job, working with the wish that your work day would be over. You will love the process of it all, and will feel excited as you greet each moment of your day.

Living this way, you will feel a deep shift inside from seeking to being.

As you feel this shift and the resulting inner peace, you will begin to glow from the inside out. That glow is the shining God-self that you are. And then you will begin to naturally attract people who are drawn to you and what you are doing.

You will gladly share all you can, and you will begin to work in harmony with others who are in similar fields of service.

As you bring through answers for humanity from God, you will find that nothing carries more ease while simultaneously bringing you deep inner joy.

Remember that it is the process and not the outcome that matters. The outcome *will* reach those who need what you are bringing through. As this begins to happen in your life, you will find that the ego's need for outer stature and status will be replaced with a simple and pure heartfelt desire to simply share. There is no amount of money that you could be offered to give up what you are doing because you will have discovered God within, and upon this discovery in the daily process of your life, you will come to feel so much inner peace and inner fulfillment that you will finally come to know what it means to be thrilled to be alive. You will feel the true life force of God working through you, in you, and as you at all times.

The radiance you will begin to feel within cannot ever be extinguished. You will be guided each moment, one step at a time, toward the next best steps to take as you are facing them. Thus, the old fears of worrying about whether or not everything is going to turn out all right will vanish.

As this happens, you will feel inspired in the moment.

Now, it may take some practice to reach this point. The best practice you can have is in bringing through answers and a higher perspective from God concerning anything in your life about which you feel a lack of inner peace. It is also crucial to address any time when you are denying or avoiding your deepest truth to yourself. The best practice is also in bringing through answers as to how to transform any view of self that still contains judgment, self-criticism, self-blame, and self-hatred. These must be uprooted and transformed. While going through this transformation on the personal level, you can certainly bring through articles, books, songs, or anything you feel inspired to create that will also reach others who are going through similar feelings and experiences.

This process can only be done in the moment. At times you may feel more physically tired because you are using all six of your senses instead of just five. The tiredness is because your energy is taken up many notches. You will need to rest as well as re-charge so your physical body can handle this charge of higher energy.

Imagine that a five-hundred-watt light bulb is suddenly placed in a lamp designed to handle only a one-hundred-watt light bulb. Some internal rewiring would be needed to handle the extra wattage. So too with your physical body. You will need to rest more and sleep more; you will then adjust to operating and living at a higher frequency.

Remember that rest and rejuvenation, relaxation, and simply recharging are just as important as doing.

Many societies and cultures place a lot of emphasis on doing. I am guiding you, however, to remember that when you rest and re-charge, you will then be able to do so much more.

Many people feel guilty when they are not constantly doing. You are not a factory assembly line, so please do not judge yourself when you need to simply clear your schedule and rest. As you rest and relax, you will find that new ideas suddenly pop into your mind. You will feel inspired as the spirit of God infuses you with new ways to reach others when you are committed to doing so from your heart. This inspiration can never be taken away from you, because its expression *is* you—you as God in physical form.

Never fear what others say. As you live and express the truth and ideas given to you, you will also come to feel a great measure of compassion for those who live with criticism and cynicism. You may remember a time, perhaps many years ago, when you were critical of others because you were unconsciously holding criticisms toward yourself. You can uproot self-criticism by asking God how to do so in your writings; then you will learn how to replace the criticism with self-truth and compassion.

Self-truth and compassion are paramount. Owning your truth gives you the courage to express it on all levels of your life, including your own unique area of service—even if this service is as simple as giving encouragement to someone who is feeling miserable—because this truth comes from your heart; it is therefore the expression of God through you.

Challenges and Society

Each person is entitled to his or her own opinion. It is important that you do not hold yourself back from expressing anything that brings your heart joy, so long as you are harming no one, including yourself, when you desire to bring your expression and life purpose out into the world.

This is why you are here in this life to begin with. It is to get in touch with your true purpose. When you live from your heart and sincerely ask God to help you either discover what your life purpose is or help you find the courage to live it in your life, you may feel afraid of what others will think. This is natural. But it is only when you live and express your truth on all levels of your life that you will feel pure inner peace as well as exhilaration and joy.

Some people are afraid of making a complete change in their life direction because of financial concerns. When you allow fear to hold you back, you perpetuate the turmoil you feel inside. Procrastination and avoidance will not bring you inner peace.

When you truly desire to take your life in the direction that your heart and soul are calling you to take, the best thing you can do is to ask God via your writings to bring you the higher perspective so that you can replace fear with certainty and courage.

Once you begin to follow the truth in your heart, you may still fear what others may say. If you find this happening in your life, simply ask God to help you work through it. Ask for the perspective that will fill you with courage so that your outer life matches the truth you feel in your heart.

Allow others their views, and at the same time remember that you are here on earth to answer to no one. You do not have a ruler or a dictator. If others judge you, simply remember that they are entitled to their views, which have nothing to do with you and are not a reflection *of* you.

Do not try to mold yourself to fit into the popular opinion of your society.

Express the best you have within you with passion, fueled by heart-centered inspiration, and then you will begin to feel an inner certainty. You will be living your truth. You will be living your life purpose, and it is important that you do not take compliments or insults too seriously. Allow neither to get to your head and inflate you or deflate you.

When God is working through you in your life purpose, there will be a time when you do, in fact, see a positive rippling effect.

You may ask God how to transform any area of your life. It all begins on the inside. Then you will have the courage to live, be, and express it all in your daily life on the outside.

Until all of humanity is living purely from the heart, without judgment, people may judge. Simply allow their judgments to float past you as you would a small cloud. Additionally, *you* may be so judgmental of yourself that it might be difficult for you to come fully into your truth. When this happens, ask God to please give you the higher perspective so that you can

transform self-judgment into self-acceptance.

Self-acceptance is required so that you
can express all of the talents, gifts, abilities,
and attributes that are uniquely yours, putting them forth as your own unique expression and purpose in this life.

Perhaps you are at a stage of life that
makes you feel you have already lived and
don't think you have the inner strength to
begin anew. If this pertains to you, simply
ask God to help you to see what you *can*
express or what views of self have caused
you to feel that your life is over, even while
you are still alive.

Finding meaning in your life and heal-
ing past hurts or past emotional pain or
self-critical views—you *can* do these things
no matter how old you may be. Evolving
and awakening to your highest view of self
remains a positive purpose of your life
regardless of your age. You do deserve to
feel your inherent worth as a pure and
beautiful soul no matter how many self-
degrading views you may still have. You can
ask God to help you transform these views,

so at least you can enjoy the remainder of your days and nights in this lifetime.

I am being guided to remind you now that there will come a time when I will no longer be in this physical life. Perhaps you are reading these words long after I have passed on.

If you *do* make a positive inner transformation in your life by asking God for answers, please do share the process with anyone who asks you how to do it.

When people see the joy you feel, when they see how you have inner peace, and when they hear wisdom flow from you, through you from God, they will be glad you were able to share the process with them.

You can ask God to have the perfect words flow into your mind to bring solace to another person who feels upset. The key is in knowing that you no longer have to do anything in your life on your own, with just your five senses.

I do promise you that when you open up and use your sixth sense consciously, you will find that the perfect words come into your mind. You will receive perfect inner guidance each moment. All you need to do is ask God to give it to you, and then it is given!

When I wake up in the morning, I ask to be consciously connected to God; I ask God to guide me each moment of my day and night. I ask this every day to remind myself that I never have to try hard for the perfect words, ideas, and guidance to flow out in my actions. I remind myself that when God, my Higher Self, works *through* me, this is using *all* of me, all six senses; and then all does flow effortlessly. This does not mean that it is always simple to take care of many areas and many details of life, but I no longer grapple trying to figure it all out. I want you to know what it feels like to live and experience each day of your life living in this manner. I want you to have *ease* when you are trying to figure something out or wondering about what the best course of action would be or what the perfect words would be for any situation facing you.

Once you ask God to give this to you, it suddenly and effortlessly flows *through* you.

When you are internally guided to move an area or aspect of your life in a certain direction, as you follow God's inner guidance, the results will appear to be what people may call miracles.

No matter what society might say about you, it is imperative that you live your truth. Then you will be a beacon for others to learn how to follow *their* truth, and fear of not being accepted or approved of will vanish. Wouldn't this be nice?

Imagine having no fear whatsoever. Imagine that you have a guarantee that everything will turn out perfectly for your highest good and for the highest good of all. *This* is what will happen when you live consciously, asking God for answers, guidance, and direction.

Your life will transform.

The rippling effect will reach others in vastly positive ways. Problems that used to plague humanity in different societies will be resolved and transformed. All because you had the heartfelt desire to make a difference in your own life, and then got so excited about it that you just began to share it with others. This is what happens when people live guided from within by God.

Many decades ago, when the telephone was invented, many people felt they didn't need this expensive new method of communication. The same thing happened when the cellular phone was invented. The people who invented them, and the people who got so excited about discovering the new inventions, wanted to share these methods and spread the word about how wonderful they really were to help make communication in life easier for others.

Why am I addressing this? You may wonder, so I will share the answer with you now.

Many people still think it is impossible to receive answers directly from God. At the time of this writing, there are pockets of people around the world whose lives have been or are being completely transformed because they learned exactly how to ask God for answers. I guided each of them to simply share the process in their own words, from their heart, in their own unique way, to help others with this "new" method of communication, although it is far from new. It is built into every human being who ever lived.

It does astound me how the masses of people living on this planet have not been taught this in the thousands of years since the time of Moses to our modern times. Perhaps there were other civilizations who knew this but no longer exist. I would venture to say that this is how the pyramids of Egypt were built. I would venture to say that those people did, in fact, have direct communication with God on the conscious level to be able to build the pyramids without electricity and sophisticated machines.

So now, in this era, as humanity has taken a huge leap in technological advances, our communication with God must take this same leap to bring about the immense catalysts for positive, heart-centered advances among the human populous. This is necessary to keep humanity from destroying itself with technology used by people who have not yet learned how to live from their hearts.

This is why it is so important for humanity to know exactly how to receive answers, guidance, clarification, and direction directly from God. It is so that heart-centered truth can flourish and match the technological advances that will prove to be extremely beneficial for humanity when everybody is living with pure motives.

When you *do* bring through answers and information from God, either in speech, in your writing, in your dreams, or in your creative endeavors, you will find that truth comes to the surface. As a result, you will ultimately decide that anything not of truth must either be eliminated from your life or transformed.

You may find that you outgrow certain people. This does not mean that one person is better than another; it simply means that when a person comes fully into his or her truth, he or she will prefer to associate with people who are also living purely with their truth rather than with fear, denial, or ill motives. This is also why people will no longer tolerate remaining miserable in relationships in which abuse, criticisms, and harsh treatment prevail.

When you come into your truth it will be reflected in all of your actions, and you will become an unstoppable force of good in this world. Additionally, you will no longer allow other people to walk all over you or manipulate you. You will become quite discerning about who you will allow in your life. If you pick up on motives from others that are not of the highest integrity, you will have the inner truth and courage to simply remove yourself from those people. In a nutshell, you will not take any bull from anyone, ever. You will not allow yourself to compromise your ethics for societal stature or success because your feelings of worth will come from within.

If there is any part of your life that you feel unhappy about, now is the time to ask God to help you process it and understand how to view it. The higher perspective you bring through from God will greatly help you find the inner strength to transform it completely.

When People Are Afraid of Receiving the Truth from God

Some people who have brought through 1,000 percent accurate information, answers, guidance, and direction in their writings from God chose to *not* bring through this information any more because if they continued to do so, they would have to face their *entire* truth on every level of their life. People in unhappy relationships who are afraid of being alone or who are afraid of making positive life changes may choose to remain in their familiar comfort zone and continue as they did in the past, despite their unhappiness.

Why would people do this? You may wonder. The answer is that even positive change can feel scary. In fact, change does feel scary many times. If you should ever find that you are afraid of change, the best thing you can do is to ask God in your writings to continue to give you answers and higher perspective to help you move to the other side of your fears and into life-enhancing action. Another excellent way to achieve this transformation is to ask God to bring you new realizations during your sleep, so upon waking up you have an entirely new perspective that will bring you the inner courage you did not feel before.

You have to *ask* God for this with a sincere and willing heart. God will *never* interfere with a person's free will and choice. Only if people are *willing* to create positive change and transformation will the answers and information come to them, and to you.

No Interference from God

Humanity has been and always will be endowed with free will and choice.

Each person who ever lived or who is alive today carries the life force of God within. Now you may wonder about people who have committed atrocities against other human beings. Those people did so out of their own free will and choice. Alternatively, people who bring forth dramatically positive differences for others also do so out of their free will and choice. There is cause and effect, however, and people's motives and actions are returned to them many times over.

The reason God does not interfere with your free will and choice is so that you can choose to evolve, choose to be and express your God-self. This is the reason you came into this life. Once you do become more consciously awakened by activating your sixth sense and your conscious communication with God, then you will be completely aware of the fact that you are guided internally by God each moment you are alive.

You might remember a time in your own life when you did or said something unkind; you always had the free will and choice to continue on the same path or to turn things around for the better.

God does not judge you. "Judgment" is simply cause and effect. God does not punish people. "Punishment" comes when a person acts out of harmful motives, which then are returned to that person multiplied; although it may appear as if God brought His or Her wrath upon that person, this is *not* the case. How could God be perfect love, purity, light, and truth as well as darkness, judgment, harm, and pain? This would mean that God had duality. And this is *not* the essence of God. There is *no* duality.

Human beings do feel duality within when they are not centered in the certainty of their purest essence, their goodness, and their truth. When that is the case, their inner duality comes out in their actions and causes harm to or judgment of self or others. This is what humanity must grow out of, through spiritual evolution, through discovering the truth by asking God for answers, so truth and purity of motives can override false views of self and destructive motives.

God does not judge. And yet, I know in my own life I used to be quite critical about myself, put myself down, and compare myself to others. When I did this, I usually felt at the bottom of the comparison chart. When I had low self-worth, and extremely low self-esteem, *that* was when I used to judge others. Once I began receiving answers and guidance from God to help me learn *how* to turn around low self-worth, I discovered that I completely stopped judging others as well, and I replaced judgment with loving compassion.

I can assure you that when you see other people judge and try to control others, they are doing so because of their own insecurity and low self-worth. There is such a thing called putting ourselves in other people's shoes. We need to remember that when others lash out, they are usually experiencing emotional pain, low self-esteem, and inner turmoil.

Whenever you feel that you are suffering, all you need to do is ask God how to turn it around. Now, if each person alive did this, and if all internal suffering, emotional pain, and low self-worth was transformed, then I am sure you would agree humanity as a whole would experience heaven on earth.

I can promise you that if I could go from feeling the lowest feelings of self-recrimination, self-hate, and self-degradation and turn them all around through God's guidance as to exactly how to do that for myself, then you can, too.

Once you do, all you will feel is pure inner peace. Once you feel pure inner peace, you will no longer feel you have to prove yourself to anyone, and you will no longer feel you have to prove your worth even to our own self. You will simply be and express who you are with joy and inner peace as well as compassion for all others who do not yet feel this same way.

Transforming Views of Self

Many of us have false negative views of self that we took on as a result of experiences in this life. Those perceptions can be completely transformed. Simply write to God and ask how to view yourself. Ask God any question you have from your heart. Ask God to give you the higher and more truthful perspective concerning any and every single area in which your view of self is less than goodness, and any area in which you feel fear. If you are earnest about it, you will receive the higher perspective. It will take conscious effort on your part to integrate the new views and to become consciously aware of the thoughts that go through your mind. A good rule of thumb is to notice any time you feel upset. Then take stock and ask yourself to become consciously aware of the thoughts that have been going through your mind.

Are you angry at someone? Do you feel that others are not treating you well? Are you fearful of leaving or being in a relationship? If you feel any of the above, ask God to give you the higher perspective that will summon your inner strength to become aware of what has been holding you back so you can live your *real* truth.

This is the part of personal transformation that the ego fears on the five-sensory personality level. Moving out of your comfort zone and into your truth may feel scary, but it is the only way to feel inner peace. No one can do this for you but you. No one can give you inner peace because the root cause of inner peace is the perceptions that you hold in your mind.

Therefore, if your mind is filled with fear, doubt, and uncertainty, consider this: by receiving answers directly from God because your heart so deeply wants them, you can receive the perspective that will shift your mind's view from perceptions that cause you to feel emotional pain to perceptions that cause you to feel emotional peace.

This responsibility is solely yours. No one can force you to do this. No one can force you to honor your truth and follow through in your actions. I can assure you and even guarantee that once you do follow through with the truth in your heart, the fear will dissipate and inner peace will prevail.

It is important that you do have tremendous patience with yourself, especially if you are transforming a lifetime of feeling everything other than inner peace. Outer conditions cannot ever bring you permanent inner peace.

If you believe that any thing or condition outside of you will be a permanent source of inner joy and peace, then you will forever be chasing after something to try to control the conditions outside of you. I used to live this way, and when I did, I was always worried about outcomes. My mind was always focused on the future. I didn't have a clue about what inner peace felt like *until* I integrated the guidance I received from God in my writings and the inner transformations were made.

The outer conditions about which you feel dissatisfied, and the people who act unkindly toward you are actually catalysts that move you to take personal responsibility to create the changes in your life that you really prefer. By asking God for help with this process, you will be pleasantly surprised at the difference the answers you receive will make in your life as long as you follow through in your actions.

When you begin to value yourself enough to want to authentically empower yourself, and love yourself, you will come to find, as I have found, that God is and will forever be your unfailing source of guidance and answers.

Once you begin to ask God for guidance and answers, especially about how to turn around any aspect of your views of yourself and any condition in your life that you do not prefer, you will come to trust this process, and you will come to the realization that God will always steer you in the direction that is for your highest good and in the direction that reflects your deepest and highest truths.

The most fantastic part of this process is that it is completely free of charge and available to you with every breath you take for as long as life itself exists. Now, how's *that* for a reliable source?

Nothing comes close. Nothing!

I can only share with you about my own process, and I do hope that in doing so, a spark of hope, inspiration, and a sense of life renewal will ignite within you. I can only promise you that when you do ask from your heart, you will be answered.

As you grow and evolve in your life, your outer circumstances will change to reflect the growth, realizations, and truth you are living on the inside.

Nothing in this universe can ever extinguish God's unfailing love for you and connection to you. There is no separation between you and God. Remember this any time you have a gut feeling. It didn't fall out of the sky like an asteroid from outer space and hit you on the head; it came from God's life force within you. It is your sixth sense. No one can see it or touch it or interfere with it, ever. Only you can feel it, and when you do, I strongly urge you to follow it with pure trust. I know you will be so glad you did.

There is still another aspect about receiving answers from God that I would like to share with you, and this is about receiving answers for other people.

Please now turn the page, and the answers will be there for you in the next chapter.

Receiving Answers from God for Other People

When people know that you are receiving answers from God, there might come a time when someone asks you for answers for themselves.

The very best thing you can do in this situation is to bring through a loving message of support and encouragement from God for them, and then share with them how they can receive answers for themselves.

There might be certain times, however, when you receive a lifesaving warning from God for another person. This is always accompanied by a strong gut feeling. The reason the strong gut feeling is there is to get you to notice it, so you can share the information with the person in order save his or her life.

This has nothing to do with being psychic, and this has nothing to do with future predictions. You will always receive a life-saving warning in the moment that it is needed simply because it will save a person's life. When you do, no matter how silly you may feel, it is important that you do pass what you received to the other person.

I am going to share a real life example for you, so that you can better understand.

Several years ago, one of my colleagues, Gary Renard, was traveling by airplane to many different cities to talk about his book.

I had a gut feeling of uneasiness about his flying the next day. I had a very strong gut feeling that he should not take the flight he was booked on but that he should wait and travel the following day instead. I felt embarrassed to send him an e-mail telling him this, and I simply wished him a safe flight. My insecure ego, my fear of looking like a fool, got in the way, and I didn't tell him about the strong gut feeling

I had. That night, I had terrible dreams of his airplane not taking off, and then saw him in my dreams taking several different flights, landing in different cities.

I awoke early in the morning and the words of God came into my mind and told me to do everything I could to contact him and advise him not to get on the airplane he was booked on. I e-mailed him several times, called his home phone and cell phone, but couldn't reach him. I felt a horrific sinking feeling that was so dreadful, I nearly fainted. I then went to sleep because I couldn't bare my feelings, couldn't stand the fact that I didn't tell him the night before and that now I couldn't reach him. I realized that at this point there was nothing more I could do. So I prayed very hard to keep him safe.

I woke up several hours later, and the words of God came into my mind and told me that he was okay. I felt an immediate sense of great relief from the horror I had felt hours earlier.

Late that night, he called me. He told me that when the flight he was booked on, the same one that I had a warning about, was on the runway about to take off, something happened to the engine. If they had taken off, the plane would have crashed. Then, just as it was shown to me in my sleep, he had to take several planes and landed in different cities until he reached his intended destination. Needless to say, it was a horrible day of traveling for him.

He confirmed everything that God showed me in my sleep, the words that came into my mind, and the message that he was okay.

I knew from that point foreword, no matter how silly I might feel, I could not withhold lifesaving information from someone, and I never have since that time. Now, the only reason I am sharing this with you is because once you begin to receive answers from God on the conscious level, you might also receive guidance that could very well save someone's life or keep them from having a very unpleasant experience, such as a miserable day of traveling, when all would go smoothly the next day.

You *will* receive pictures or words that come into your mind, and strong feelings in the middle of your stomach or maybe in your chest. You will notice the feelings because they will be strong.

It is important to share such information solely to bring lifesaving guidance to the person you received the information about.

Your head may doubt if it is real. You may feel insecure or embarrassed to share what you receive, just as I did. But sharing it is more important than withholding it out of fear of looking or sounding foolish.

I am going to give you one more example so you can understand how this information will come to you in the moment.

By this time I had learned my lesson about not *censoring* what I was receiving from God.

No, this does not make me a crystal ball psychic. God gives messages to us *all*; we just need to pay attention to them and *listen*.

While I was holding a private telephone session with a client who was pregnant, I kept getting a picture of her throwing a white, goose-down comforter over her bed. Along with this picture, I received images in my mind of her vacuuming her house and taking the garbage out.

What I was "getting" or receiving from God was to tell her to stop lifting the heavy goose-down comforter, and to stop vacuuming and taking the garbage out, because each time she did, she was putting pressure on her uterus and could have a miscarriage.

Now, I knew as much about her daily chores and what type of blanket she had on her bed as I do about yours. I knew nothing. But I did share this information with her, because what comes from God is pure and will always be for a person's highest good.

She was quite surprised, as I was, that everything I shared with her was exactly correct. For all I knew, she could have had a crocheted quilt from her great grandmother on her bed. But she did have a heavy goose-down comforter, and she was vacuuming two times each day, as well as taking out the trash. I guided her to stop because this is what God guided me to share with her. As a result, a miscarriage was prevented.

Warnings to save people's lives just pop into your mind in the moment. It is not something that you can predict, and the *last* thing I will guide you to do is to start predicting things for people, because this is more disempowering than empowering.

But a lifesaving warning is something you would feel much better passing along rather than not passing along.

If you are teaching other people how to receive answers from God, it is so important that you allow the information to flow into your mind, and simply share what you are receiving.

Whenever I teach this to people, before our sessions, I "get" within my mind the words of God and what the people are struggling with in regard to their Higher Self communication. I receive such things as what they are afraid of; what issues they need to focus on now, in the moment, to guide them to the next level.

People are not used to this level of communication, just as I was not when I first began. It is natural for us to think we are making it all up. It is natural to think we might be getting it wrong. These fears arise simply because we have not yet had enough practice to trust receiving answers from God. We have been conditioned to live according to what our five senses show us.

Trust comes over time and through many small experiences.

If you wish to bring through information for others, please do so only in a manner that will guide them to continue to bring through the answers from God for themselves.

With each client, I *always* say, "When you have a gut feeling, do not listen to what I say, do not listen to what anybody says; always follow what your gut feelings are telling you because this is God speaking to you, and God will never lie to you." I share with all of my clients that bringing through information either for themselves or for others must be done solely with the motive to be of help and service and to *never, ever* make a person dependent on *you* for answers when they can simply depend on God.

What you *can* bring through are things such as the words of God that are flowing into your mind, and analogies to help authentically *empower* other people to rise above their fears about whether they are getting it right.

Asking for answers from God *must be done only from the heart.* This is *not* an intellectual exercise. This is *not* a special ability, either. It is no more a special ability than having a gut feeling. It is the *heartfelt desire* that establishes the conscious connection to receive answers from God. This is not for the purpose of making predictions. This is *only* for the purpose of personal evolution, positive personal transformation, and then for the purpose of bringing through information to be of pure heart-centered service to humanity. You can also be of pure heart-centered service to animals, plant life, the environment, or any part of life on earth that truly means something to you in your *heart.*

Teaching this to others is best done after you have had much practice bringing through information that has resulted in your own profound and positive life transformation. After *you* have had much practice, *then* you can *share* it with other people from your heart.

The whole purpose of this book is to share the process with all of humanity. Eventually, the book will be published in Braille. Meanwhile, if you are teaching the process to people who cannot read because of blindness, you can read it to them. They can learn how to bring through the information in the way that's easiest for them, which will most likely be through words flowing into their minds that they can speak into a voice recording device

People who are deaf can be taught this process through sign language.

All people, even those without one or more of the five physical senses, can learn this. Everyone alive receives information from God. Heightened intuition *is* God communicating with everyone, through strong gut feelings. Every person has them. It is important that you do not try to have people follow you but that you guide them to authentically empower themselves by receiving their own answers directly.

I guide my clients in as short a time as possible, because I will never allow anyone to become dependent on *me* when the one they will do much better becoming consciously at one with is God—which is the essence of each person's life force, heart, and soul.

How to Tell When Ego Has Taken Over

If you are either doing this for yourself or are teaching it to others, the surest way to tell if the information is coming from ego is when you hear an intellectual process, with a lot of "shoulds" along with judgment. All of this comes from ego.

When you are teaching another person how to bring through answers from God, it is important that you share that it is actually the most simple process. It feels *effortless.* It flows naturally. The fact that it does flow so naturally is the main reason that I and everyone I have ever shared this with thought at first that we were making it up.

The answers from God are always simple, yet with unconditionally loving higher wisdom. For example, when you ask about personal transformation for self-worth, guidance about your career or your life purpose, or when you ask for answers about the best course of action, the answers will be simple.

There were literally thousands of times when God guided me to "live in the moment," "love yourself," "trust that everything will work out according to what is for your highest good," as well as the biggie for me that took about three years for me to finally get and live in my everyday life, which was "go with the flow."

I cannot tell you how difficult that was for me! God would many times let me know that "the truth is persistent, and it does not change."

There were so many times I would receive the same answers over and over again, until I finally integrated the answers and actually lived the messages.

Trusting, going with the flow, loving myself, living in the moment: how elusive this state of being and living is until we get it, and finally learn how to live it. The only way I can guide you to live this way is to advise you to write to God and ask God to give you the analogies, answers, guidance, direction, and clarification that you can relate to so that it reaches you. One of the best things to do is to re-read or repeat the answers until they are integrated and you are living with inner peace.

Perhaps you know someone who is falling apart emotionally because of a severely difficult traumatic event. If you *really* and truly want to help, share how to ask God for the higher reasons behind the trauma, and for the higher perspective, so that God can help the person transform from feeling emotionally crushed to feeling a renewed sense of hope and a reason to be alive, much like my own transformation that I shared earlier in this book.

When you teach a person how to bring through answers for themselves, you are doing a great service. Never judge other people with respect to their personal growth. Everyone is doing the best job they know how to do at any given time.

Encourage people to ask God directly, rather than asking other people for their opinions. God will always give each person divine, pure, and perfect truth.

When God Works Through You for Others

You might be reading this book now either because you already know you are going to help people learn this process or to prepare yourself for the point in your life when deep in your heart you will feel and know that you are, in fact, working for God. As you live and share this process, you will feel at one with God and will feel God working through you to reach other people no matter what field of service you are engaged in. All service from the heart is sacred and blessed. There will always be people who need what you can share with them, from God, through you.

For example, you might be drawn to help the elderly or children. Someone else might be drawn to help people who have been raped or experienced incest. Other people might be drawn to help war veterans. Others might be drawn to help homeless people.

I have found that the areas in which we have personally experienced the greatest challenges in our own lives are typically the areas to which we feel most drawn to serve and help uplift others who are going through similar challenges.

Since I have never served in a war, I could not personally relate, share, or be most effective to help people who have experienced the horrors of war.

I am being guided to share this with you because there *is* a higher reason why you have had or are having specific challenges in your life: so that you can transform it for yourself and then help other people who are going through similar experiences to also transform their deepest challenges into their greatest strengths and areas of personal service.

You might be the parent of a child who is not physically well. You might be searching for answers. Once you begin to ask God for guidance and answers, you can begin to receive them. As a result of the difference asking makes in your own life, you might decide that you would like to share the process with other parents you meet or become friends with.

The same is true for every area of life and for every challenge. When you look back on how you have transformed what was once your greatest challenge, you may very well feel a calling in your heart to help uplift the lives of others in your own unique way. You might want to write a song that brings hope and inspiration.

You might question your life direction and ask yourself what means something to you in your heart. Then, as you are guided by God to follow the truth in your heart, you become a beacon of hope, life renewal, and inspiration for yourself and for others.

So much good comes from receiving answers directly from God. The immeasurable difference it will make in your life will be in exact accordance with your steadfast, earnest, and heartfelt desire to truly transform every false, disempowering view or belief that has been holding you back.

When you are receiving answers from God, you will discover, as surely as the sun rises each day, that there is no condition you cannot overcome. The condition I am speaking of is how you view the situation, your perception about what is truth, and learning from God about any limiting beliefs you may still have that are holding you back on any level.

Once your view shifts to the highest perspective, then phenomenal, life-enriching and vastly positive transformations are made. The transformations all take place within your mind. The higher perspective to help you transform comes from God. Integrating the new, life-enhancing perspective comes with focusing on it rather than on one that is life-depleting.

All of this is within your free will and choice.

You can ask for answers, or you can choose to never ask.

One thing is certain: when God works *through* you, you are *not* "giving up" your free will and choice. What you *are* doing is working with *all* of your senses. All of you combined will prove to be far more effective than only part of you.

I would like to ask you a few questions now.

Would you like any problem you are facing to be transformed?

Would you like to live a life of *permanent* inner peace and joy?

Would you like to feel pure self-love and acceptance, and simultaneously feel passionately alive?

I used to feel the exact opposite of all of the above, as I have shared with you. If my life could be completely transformed from being at the brink of suicide to feeling genuine self-love and pure inner peace, and being passionately alive, your life can, too.

No matter what is weighing on your heart or on your mind, there *is* an answer. Ask God to help you see the higher perspective. Ask what you can do to begin to transform anything you feel a lack of inner peace about. Ask why! Ask any and every question you have until you have every answer you need. Keep asking God to guide you.

Keep asking God to help you work through any feeling or circumstance you feel unhappy about.

Ask God to help you with any fears you have.

Ask God what the best course of action would be for your highest good and the highest good of all.

You will receive simple answers. But if you find them hard to follow, then ask God to give you a realization so that you can gain the inner courage to follow your deepest truth. If you falter, I can assure you God does have the most unlimited patience I have ever experienced. If you do not follow the answers you receive, remember there is no judgment. The answers will always guide you to follow your deepest truth.

The truth, *your deepest* truth, will free you from *anything* that has been holding you back. What God brings to you is always truth.

If you wonder whether God hears you, and if you would like an answer, trust that you will receive it. And no matter how many times you need to hear or receive the same answers, you will always be lovingly supported until you feel the courage to follow your truth in your words and actions based on the deepest truth in your heart.

There is only one thing I must give you fair warning about, and this I give to you with a smile. Expect to be heard, answered, and most of all, expect to see your life transform on all levels so profoundly that you will look back and feel that it has been a miracle.

It truly has been a miracle, and that miracle is your awareness of God always with you, working and being in you, as you, and through you.

The greatest miracle of it all is the joy you are going to feel when you come to know that God views *you* as the miracle. It is because of you that a beacon of light— your light, your courage, your purity of motives, and your heartfelt sharing—is going to touch the lives of others. Then you will see the rippling effect, and you will understand what it means to be a living expression of God.

That is what you are. If you question this, ask God. I promise you that you will always receive an answer, and that answer will always take you into the fabric of your being which is the purest and most beautiful creation on earth. That is why there is only one you.

Now, if you wish, discover all your heart yearns to discover, and remember to love the process of your discovery. The process of simply being, expressing, asking, sharing, and remembering that you are never alone for as long as life exists.

God is always with you, and when you doubt this fact, just ask. I guarantee you will always be answered, and the answers will always bring you into your deepest heart, where pure truth dwells and will live on for eternity.

Love, trust, ask, express, create, share, rest, and always, under all circumstances, follow the truth in your heart—because that is where God always is.

About the Author

 Barbara Rose, Ph.D., most widely known as "Born To Inspire," is a best-selling author and internationally recognized expert in personal transformation, relationships and spiritual awakening. She is a pioneering force in incorporating Higher Self Communication the study and integration of humanity's God-Nature into modern personal growth and spiritual evolution.

Her highly acclaimed books, public speaking events, tele-seminars, internationally published articles and intensives have transformed the lives of thousands across the globe.

Known for providing life-changing answers, quick practical coaching and deep spiritual wisdom to people worldwide she is the founder of IHSC – Institute of

Higher Self Communication, *inspire!* magazine, and Rose Humanitarian Alliance.

Barbara works in cooperation with some of the greatest spiritual leaders of our time to uplift the spiritual consciousness of humanity. Visit her website at www.borntoinspire.com.

Printed in the United States
60599LVS00001B/157-159